Careers for
TECH GIRLS IN
E-COMMERCE

JACKSON NIEUWLAND

Rosen
YA™
New York

Published in 2019 by The Rosen Publishing Group, Inc.
29 East 21st Street, New York, NY 10010

Library of Congress Cataloging-in-Publication Data

Names: Nieuwland, Jackson, author.
Title: Careers for tech girls in e-commerce / Jackson Nieuwland.
Description: New York : Rosen Publishing, 2019 | Series: Tech girls |
Audience: Grades 7–12. | Includes bibliographical references and index.
Identifiers: LCCN 2017049225| ISBN 9781508180173 (library bound) | ISBN 9781508180180 (pbk.)
Subjects: LCSH: Electronic commerce—Vocational guidance—Juvenile literature. | Women in marketing—Juvenile literature.
Classification: LCC HF5415.35 .N54 2018 | DDC 381/.142023—dc23
LC record available at https://lccn.loc.gov/2017049225

Manufactured in the United States of America

CONTENTS

Introduction

ack in the early nineties, buying a book was a lot harder than it is today. First, you went to your local bookstore and looked through the shelves for the specific title you wanted. If the store didn't have it, you'd check a few more bookstores, hoping one of them stocked it. Then, if none of the bookstores in your area had the book, you'd have to get one of them to order it in. This could take a few weeks. When the store finally gave you the call to let you know your book had arrived, you had to go back into town to pick it up.

Then, in July 1995, everything changed. That's when Amazon launched. Back then, Amazon only sold books, but now the company has gone way beyond that, selling almost anything you can imagine: clothes, furniture, makeup, food, electronics … the list goes on. And Amazon isn't the only company selling things online. E-commerce is now a huge part of the global marketplace, accounting for 8.7 percent of retail sales in 2016, according to a Statista report. That figure was expected to increase to 15.5 percent by 2021.

But just because you don't have to go up to the counter and hand bills and coins to a cashier to buy things anymore doesn't mean that these purchases happen magically, with no one working behind the scenes. According to *Forbes*, between 2007 and 2017, the e-commerce industry created 355,000

Amazon is the largest e-retailer in the United States, with more than 310 million active users. The company shipped an estimated 1.6 million packages a day in 2017.

new jobs in the United States, including positions in warehousing, customer service, and, of course, technology. The three main tech jobs in the world of e-commerce are market research analysts, web developers, and computer systems analysts, all of which make great careers for young women.

Forbes also reports that women are bigger users of e-commerce than men, with 70 to 80 percent of all consumer purchasing being driven by women. That means that even when a product isn't being bought *by* a woman, it's probably being bought *for* one or at the suggestion of one. Considering this information, it seems shocking that only 12 percent of e-commerce CEOs are women. How can these companies hope to understand and cater to their customers if they don't employ people from the demographics to which they're selling?

A 2016 study by the Peterson Institute for International Economics found that the more women a company has in leadership roles, the more successful that company will be. So why not start on your journey to working in e-commerce now? The industry needs you!

Chapter one

WHAT IS E-COMMERCE AND WHAT DOES IT HAVE TO DO WITH ME?

E-commerce is pretty easy to define. It is simply the act of buying and selling online. The first things most people think of when they hear this definition are websites that sell physical products to consumers, like Pizza Hut, Asos, or Overstock. Some of these companies have physical storefronts as well as online stores, but they aren't the only types of businesses covered by the term "e-commerce." There are websites that allow users to sell their own products, like eBay, Etsy, or Big Cartel. There are apps that allow customers to pay for services, like Uber, Fiverr, and Postmates. There are companies that sell products that only exist digitally, like Squarespace, Spotify, and Adobe Creative Cloud. There are even services designed to allow you to send money to other people without necessarily receiving anything in return, like Paypal, Venmo, and Square Cash. Basically, if you can imagine a monetary transaction that could happen online, it comes under the umbrella of e-commerce.

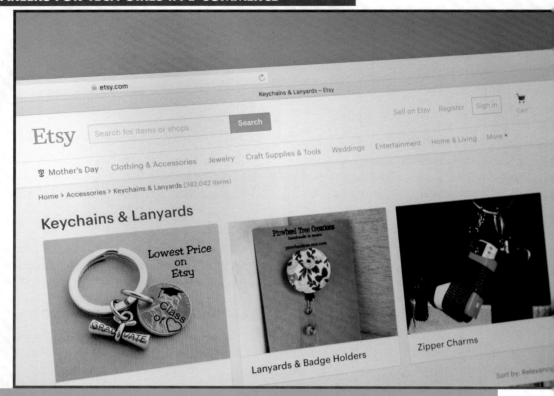

Platforms like Etsy (www.etsy.com) make it easy for people to set up their own online stores without having to learn how to code.

TYPES OF E-COMMERCE

Even though there are many different kinds of products and services available to consumers through e-commerce, these transactions only make up a fraction of the e-commerce industry. It's not just individual people who are buying things online; it's also businesses and even governments paying for services. Since e-commerce includes so many different types of transactions, it can be difficult to keep track of everything it includes. The most common way of categorizing the different types of e-commerce is by identifying who is selling to whom.

BUSINESS TO CONSUMER

This is the most well-known form of e-commerce to most of us because these retailers market to us as consumers. It makes sense that we don't know the names of businesses that provide services to the government because they don't need us to know about them (their audience is the government), but if we as consumers didn't know about a company like Grubhub, that would be a problem for Grubhub.

BUSINESS TO BUSINESS

People usually think of businesses as providers of goods and services to individual consumers, but in a lot of transactions, businesses are actually selling things to other businesses. For example, most businesses have offices, and offices need supplies like paper, pens, folders, and other stationery, so companies like Staples make a lot of sales to other businesses. Some companies like Podio, a project management software company, don't even sell to individual consumers at all. They base their entire business on catering to the needs of other companies.

E-Commerce makes it easy for businesses to restock their office supplies. When they're running low on something, they can place an order within minutes.

CONSUMER TO CONSUMER (C2C)

C2C is another well-known and popular form of e-commerce. It is made up of services that allow users to sell to other users. This includes well-known websites like Craigslist and Depop. Most people use these services to sell things they no longer want or to make a little extra money on the side from a hobby, but some people actually manage to make a living using this form of e-commerce.

CROWDFUNDING

Crowdfunding holds a unique place in the e-commerce industry. It can fit into both the business-to-consumer and consumer-to-consumer categories, but the interesting thing is that, for the most part, crowdfunding doesn't involve people buying things. It involves people either investing in or donating to things.

Although the concept of crowdfunding dates back hundreds of years, the first documented online crowdfunding platform was ArtistShare, a website founded in 2001 that allows fans to help fund musicians' projects. ArtistShare's first project was Maria Schneider's album *Concert in the Garden* (2004), which went on to win the Grammy for Best Large Jazz Ensemble Album. Since then, crowdfunding has exploded with the launch of a seemingly endless array of sites, including platforms like Kickstarter, Indiegogo, and GoFundMe.

Although there are plenty of general crowdfunding platforms, there are also a lot of specialist platforms, designed to raise money for specific kinds of projects. StartSomeGood is just for social change initiatives. Appbackr lets mobile developers raise funds to build apps. Seed&Spark helps filmmakers raise money for their next movies or TV shows. Cruzu is all about wine making.

Different platforms also have different rules. Some require projects to reach their funding goals in order to keep any of the money they raise, while others let them keep the funds even if they don't reach their goals. Some offer rewards for contributions, while others depend on the charity of donations.

(continued on the next page)

(continued from the previous page)

Some platforms will accept any and every project, while others are more selective. And, of course, different platforms take a higher or lower percentage of the funds raised.

There is a crowdfunding platform out there for every project, no matter how obscure. If you're interested in e-commerce, running this sort of campaign can be a good way to dip your toes in the water.

BUSINESS TO GOVERNMENT

As well as buying from other businesses, companies also need to pay the government for various things, including taxes, licensing, certification, and more. Most of these transactions now take place online, and many of them are even automated so that no one at the company has to go through the tedious process of making a payment every time.

GOVERNMENT TO BUSINESS

Even the government needs to pay for things. There are many things the government needs done for which it doesn't have dedicated staff, so it hires outside contractors to do the work. Also, like businesses, it needs office supplies, vehicles, computers, and other products, which it buys from companies, often paying over the internet.

E-commerce is useful because it allows you to purchase things from wherever you are, as long as you have access to a phone (or other device) and credit card.

CONSUMER TO GOVERNMENT

People transfer money to the government all the time through taxes, paying fines, applications for various licenses, and more. In the past, these sorts of payments used to be made in person using cash or by mailing a check or a credit card form. Now, most of these transactions are completed online, a much faster and more convenient process.

GOVERNMENT TO CONSUMER

The government also sends money in the other direction, to individual people, in the form of retirement, unemployment, and disability benefits, for example. Performing these transactions online is much more reliable than past methods. For people living from benefit check to benefit check, it's a big deal if a check gets lost in the mail. But when the process happens online, they don't have to worry about that.

WHERE YOU FIT IN

All of these forms of e-commerce require people to fill three specific tech positions: market research analysts, developers, and computer systems analysts. The demand for all three of these jobs is growing at an above-average rate, with new positions being created all around the world on a daily basis. The company you end up working for might not even exist yet, but if you start preparing for a career in e-commerce now, you'll be ready by the time it does.

MARKET RESEARCH ANALYSTS

This job is all about figuring out who your company should be trying to sell its products to and how best to get those people to buy these products. It involves a lot of research and interpreting data. If you're interested in statistics or marketing, this might be a good career for you.

WEB DEVELOPERS

If you're interested in the websites and apps themselves, then web development is probably the direction in which you want to head. These jobs focus on building the systems that allow e-commerce transactions to take place. Web developers use coding languages to design webstores. They design the page layouts, site navigation, drop-down menus, and credit card forms. Not only that but they build

If you're confident using the internet and new forms of technology, then you could do well pursuing a career in e-commerce.

all the behind-the-scenes systems that make the websites and transactions work. If you're interested in design or programming, this might be the career for you.

COMPUTER SYSTEMS ANALYSTS

Web developers build the e-commerce platforms, and computer systems analysts help businesses use that technology efficiently. They set up computer systems, selecting the most beneficial hardware and software so their company is always operating at an optimal level; they identify possible problems and fix bugs that are reported to them; and they keep up to date with the latest technology so that they are always ready to upgrade and improve their company's system. If you enjoy problem solving and get excited about new technology, then you'll make a great computer systems analyst.

Chapter two

MARKET RESEARCH ANALYSTS: PERSUADING PEOPLE TO BUY THINGS

Marketing has always been a part of commerce, from which stallholder could shout the loudest at the market to junk mail pamphlets to sponsoring sports teams, but as more and more businesses and transactions move online, the way companies try to reach their audiences changes. E-commerce generates huge amounts of data. Companies don't just record their customers' traditional demographics like age, gender, and location anymore. They collect extremely specific information like how you got to their websites, how long you looked at them before closing the tab, where on the screen your cursor spent the most time, and so on. They probably know your shopping habits better than you do. But all that data is of no use to them if they don't know what it means. That's where market research analysts come in.

Advertising happens everywhere, from brochures to movie product placement to sports games.

WHAT'S THE JOB?

A market research analyst's job is to use the data her company gathers and her own additional research to help the company understand both its customers' wants, needs, and spending habits, and its competitors' strategies. By analyzing this information, the analyst helps her company decide what to sell and how to best promote it to its potential customers in order to generate the most profit.

Deciding what a company should sell usually doesn't mean suggesting that it completely change what industry of which it's a part. If the analyst is working for a retail store, she might suggest different brands the shop could carry to attract more customers. If she works for a manufacturer, she would give advice about what sort of features to include in the products the company produces and whether computers should prioritize hard-drive space or processing speed, if clothes should have pockets, or if high-quality fabrics are more important.

In the same way, giving recommendations on how a business should promote its products isn't always about planning advertising campaigns. It can be as simple as where specific products are located on the website, or it could include major changes like designing a new logo. Market research analysts consider details of all sizes—whatever it takes to have an edge in the competitive marketplace.

WHAT DO THEY DO?

A market research analyst's daily tasks can be broken down into three main categories: collecting data, analyzing data, and reporting findings. These categories seem pretty simple on the surface, but there's a lot more to them than you might expect.

COLLECT DATA

There are many methods of collecting data about your customers (and potential customers): surveys, focus groups, purchase history, web traffic, and recordings of how users interact with the website. Market research analysts use all of these tools to create the fullest picture they can. Not only that, but they're also constantly coming up with new ways to gather even more useful data. If they don't keep advancing, other companies will overtake their business in the blink of an eye.

Market research analysts create graphs and diagrams like these to explain the data they gather to the other people with whom they work.

ANALYZE DATA

The amount of data generated by modern market research is staggering. Just think of how much information Facebook has about each of its users; then think about how many users Facebook has. It would take you more than ten lifetimes to go through all those numbers. So for the most part, market research analysts don't look at the habits of individual people; they look at wider trends and try to judge what they mean for their company by using graphs and other statistical models.

GIRLS RUN THE E-COMMERCE WORLD

The most important thing for any businessperson to know is her market. As e-commerce has made it easier for anyone to open up shop, many young women with strong knowledge of specific fields have used that to find success in business.

In 2011, at the age of fifteen, Tavi Gevinson founded the online magazine *Rookie.* Part of the website is an online store that sells physical anthologies of writing that previously appeared on the site and other Rookie merchandise. The venture has been a massive success. In 2015, Gevinson's net worth was estimated at $7 million.

Sophia Amoruso began her company, Nasty Gal, when she was twenty-three years old by selling vintage clothing on

(continued on the next page)

(continued from the previous page)

eBay. A year later she had her own webstore, and four years after that Nasty Gal reported revenues of almost $28 million. Although Nasty Gal has since filed for bankruptcy and Amoruso has left the company, she has still found success through her autobiography, *#GIRLBOSS*, which was turned into a television series for Netflix.

FabAlley is an Indian fashion website founded by Shivani Poddar and Tanvi Malik when they were both twenty-five years old. It quickly became one of India's most successful fashion brands. In 2016, FabAlley received $2 million in funding to further promote its growth.

Success in e-commerce can lead to opportunities in other industries. Sophia Amoruso, founder of Nasty Gal, is now a bestselling author.

REPORT FINDINGS

Lastly the analysts need to present what they've learned to the company's management. This means translating complex mathematical findings into uncomplicated diagrams and simple language. It's also not enough for them to say, "I've found that customers are spending more time reading the fine print than they used to." They need to explain what this means for the company and what specific actions they can take to make the most of this knowledge.

HOW TO PREPARE

There are a lot of skills you can work on to prepare for your career as a market research analyst. This starts at school. You'll definitely want to take math classes, particularly statistics and probability. You'll also want to focus on English. Communication is a hugely important skill in this line of work. Numbers are great, but a lot of people don't understand them, so you need to be able to translate to them. Design classes can also be helpful to give you perspective on how people interact with websites and marketing images.

One great way to kick-start your journey to a market research analyst job is to find part-time work in sales, whether that be at a clothing store or a fast food restaurant or even having your own stall at a local market. This sort of job will give you a chance to study consumer behavior and learn how to maximize sales on the micro level. You might

By the time these kids enter the workforce, they'll have developed the skills to convince both their customers and their employers that their ideas are good ones.

even earn a few bucks to put toward your college education.

Other activities that could help you on your way are joining a debate team or writing for the school newspaper. These hobbies will help you develop persuasion skills, which you'll need when making presentations to management. People won't always agree with your findings; it will be part of your job to convince them.

ACCREDITATION

Most market research analysts have at least a bachelor's degree, with some going further and getting their master's for top positions. There are a variety of disciplines that will qualify you to work as a market research analyst, including marketing, statistics, business, economics, and computer science.

In addition to university study, there is the Professional Researcher Certification offered by the Insights Association. While not mandatory, this credential, which can be applied for through the Insights Association website, highlights you as a proficient and dedicated researcher. It requires twelve hours of industry-related education, passing an exam, and twenty hours of continued education every two years to maintain the qualification.

JOB OUTLOOK

You don't need to worry that there won't be any market research analyst jobs left to fill by the time you've gotten yourself qualified. Market research analysts are required in all industries, and the jobs are being created faster than they can be filled, with employment numbers projected to increase by 23 percent between 2016 and 2026—much higher than the average increase of 7 percent, according to the Bureau of Labor Statistics' 2017 figures.

Chapter three

WEB DEVELOPERS: BUILDING THE STORE

eb developer jobs are the most glamorous in the e-commerce industry. It's the developer's work you see when you click "add to cart," and without them, e-commerce couldn't exist. Web developers build the webstores that allow monetary transactions to happen online. In the days before internet commerce, the closest role to a web developer might have been an architect who designed the store where products were sold, but even that doesn't communicate the full scope of the developer's importance to e-commerce. Not only do web developers design the stores but they also build them, create the registers, fill the shelves with products, and decorate the interior.

WHAT'S THE JOB?

Every industry needs web developers, from medicine to the military. Even ancient industries like farming make use of developers to create software to increase their efficiency. But tech industries like e-commerce are even more dependent on developers. Computers are no use unless they have software to run.

Web developers create all the software we interact with on a daily basis: the apps, the websites, even the operating systems. Building these programs requires a lot of creativity and problem solving, but e-commerce developers aren't usually given free rein on their projects. The companies they work for give them detailed outlines of what they want, and the developers have to figure out how to deliver that while also taking into account the technology hurdles that businesspeople don't usually think of.

Web developers need to build online stores that are not only efficient and intuitive but also look good to customers; otherwise, they won't get enough traffic.

Sometimes these developers will design the layout of the websites and apps themselves. Other times, they work in conjunction with designers to make the software look the best it can. Either way, they need to be able to build a platform that is not only functional but is also intuitive and draws customers in, making them want to purchase the company's products.

WHAT DO THEY DO?

Every web developer has a different skill set. Each one has different specialties, knows different programming languages, and works for a company that has different requirements. So not every developer performs the same tasks, but the process of building an e-commerce platform can be broken down into five main stages.

PLANNING

Most e-commerce development projects begin with the developer meeting with the company's management to determine what its goals are for the website or app and the scope of the project. The developer will often have to find the line between what the company wants and what it needs in order to deliver an acceptable product within the deadline and budget constraints. After the initial meeting, the developer begins work on the project, but there will be many more meetings along the way to update management on progress and any possible problems that come up.

Developers can't just make whatever websites and apps they want. They need to be able to take management's ideas and turn them into a reality.

DESIGN AND LAYOUT

Once the web developer knows what the company needs from its e-commerce platform, it's time to figure out what it will look like. Developers call this step wireframing. It is where they decide what will go on each page, how those pages will link together, and what they will look like on the screen. Depending on the developer's skill set and the company's needs, the developer may complete this stage on her own, or she may work in conjunction with a graphic designer.

CODING

It's all well and good to have designed a pretty-looking webstore, but you won't actually be able to sell anything if there's no coding behind it. This is where the actual development comes into play. There are hundreds of programming languages out there that developers use to build software. The codes they write using these languages is what makes websites and apps actually do things, rather than just being static pages. Different languages are better suited to different types of projects. Some developers specialize in one specific language, while others use many different ones.

INTEGRATE CONTENT

This is usually the easiest step for the developer. Sometimes it is even left to be done by someone else who is less tech savvy. All it involves is uploading text, images, audio, and video onto the website or app. It's almost like updating your profile picture or putting up a blog post. You've just got to make sure you put everything in the right place. You don't want a picture of a tube of toothpaste next to the link to buy superglue.

TESTING

No platform is perfect on the first try. There are always at least a few bugs and issues that need to be fixed before the site or app goes live for public consumption. Testing is usually split into two phases: alpha and beta. Alpha testing is done by the developers and the company before the platform launches to make sure it is ready for use. Beta testing happens after the platform is launched and allows users to give feedback on how the website or app could be tweaked to improve its performance.

ROSE LU: LIFE AS A WEB DEVELOPER

Rose Lu is a developer at Storypark, an online educational organization in Wellington, New Zealand.

Why did you decide to be a web developer?
I studied mechatronics engineering at university and felt mixed about it. I enjoyed software development the most. I wasn't sure I wanted to be a developer, but I thought I should try. My first job was in embedded software development, which I didn't enjoy. I moved into web development, which is more modern in the way it approaches collaboration. After two years, I felt confident I wanted to keep being a developer.

(continued on the next page)

(continued from the previous page)

What does your typical day look like?
We start with a check-in meeting where we discuss what we did yesterday, what we're doing today, and anything we need help with. Then I make coffee and catch up on messages and email. If anything needs my attention, I'll resolve that first. Next, I'll resume the piece of work I'm doing. Throughout the day I'll do code reviews, work with coworkers, and look at funny pictures on Twitter.

What's your favorite part of the job?
Software development is like a puzzle, where the clues are spread out on the internet. It can be frustrating, but it's rewarding when you solve it. It's great to create tools that help people do things they previously wouldn't have been able to do.

What challenges do you see for women in the tech industry?
The tech industry is very white, privileged, and male. At times, I've found it hard to validate my experiences because so few people could relate. It was hard to learn how to back myself and point out things that marginalize minorities. Often it wasn't worth the emotional labor. It's about finding organizations that value diversity. A key sign is the presence of women in leadership positions. If the company makes excuses about lack of candidates for those roles, they're not trying hard enough.

HOW TO PREPARE

The best way to get started with becoming a web developer is to get coding right away. This can seem intimidating at first. It's not easy to learn a new language, but there are lots of resources out there that break it down into a step-by-step process, allowing you to take your time and make sure you understand each principle before you move on to the next.

Designing websites isn't the same as designing books or flyers. You need to be able to understand and work with the underlying codes that make them operate.

Codecademy is the best known of these resources. The site offers free classes in more than ten of the most popular coding languages, including Python, Ruby, and JavaScript. But if the class structure doesn't work for you, there are plenty of other ways to learn, from YouTube tutorials to blogs to books to boot camps. Whatever your learning style, there's something out there to help you learn to code.

You can even pick up some useful basic skills by formatting posts on blogs and forums or by building games with Twine. In fact, most people who have spent a significant amount of time online have picked up a few bits of code along the way without even noticing it. Now it's just a matter of expanding on that.

ACCREDITATION

You don't technically need a degree or qualification to get a job as a web developer. The most important thing is to have good knowledge of programming languages and a strong portfolio of work that will show potential employers what you're capable of.

That being said, a qualification can certainly help you secure work, by showing your commitment to the field and separating you from your competition. The type of qualification you should pursue depends on what languages you want to learn and the sort of development work you want to do. Relevant fields of study include web design, computer science, programming, and graphic design.

Even if you don't go to college to become a developer, you'll still need to spend hours in front of a computer screen, learning coding languages and creating projects.

Throughout your career it is also important to keep up to date with new programming languages and updates to existing languages. If you fall behind the industry standards, no matter how skilled you are with the old technology, it will be hard to find work.

JOB OUTLOOK

Between 2014 and 2024 the number of web developers employed in the United States was expected to increase by 27 percent, according to the Bureau of Labor Statistics' December 2015 projections. Not only is that way above average but it is also significantly higher than those for market research analysts and computer systems analysts. This statistic includes developers in all industries, but considering the growth of e-commerce both in the United States and internationally, there's no doubt that there will be plenty of new jobs for e-commerce developers.

COMPUTER SYSTEMS ANALYSTS: MAINTAINING THE E IN E-COMMERCE

Market research analysts work primarily with data, and web developers work with code. Computer systems analysts, on the other hand, work with computers themselves. If you enjoy reading about the latest technology, comparing the specs, and setting up new systems, you might be a future computer systems analyst.

Developers design the software that makes e-commerce possible, but that software needs hardware to run on. Computer systems analysts make sure companies are running the most efficient systems and troubleshoot any operational problems that come up. They usually work with a system over an extended period of time, rather than just setting it up and moving on.

WHAT'S THE JOB?

It costs a lot of money to set up an IT (information technology) system. There are computers, servers, accessories, software, and more to account for. To make sure that investment isn't wasted, companies employ computer systems analysts to optimize their systems using cost-benefit analyses and extensive tech knowledge.

These analysts need to understand computer systems inside and out. They have to understand how each and every component operates as a part of the whole and whether those parts are being used as efficiently as possible or if there are different components that would work better in their place.

Most people shouldn't take machines apart—they could damage the hardware or hurt themselves—but for computer systems analysts, it's all in a day's work.

They use this knowledge to build systems specifically tailored to the companies that employ them or to improve those companies' existing systems.

They also need to be able to identify what is causing problems with a system, fix those problems, and prevent them from occurring again.

WHAT WAS THE FIRST THING EVER SOLD ONLINE?

Nowadays you can buy anything you like online, but as recently as the early nineties, e-commerce didn't exist at all. What was the beginning of this explosion of internet purchasing? There are a lot of ideas about what the first e-commerce transaction was but only one true answer.

One theory is that the first online purchase happened in 1984, when Jane Snowball, a seventy-four-year-old British grandma, ordered groceries from her local store using Videotex, a technology that involved connecting a TV to telephone lines to send text. However, the payment was made in cash when the groceries were delivered, so the transaction didn't technically happen online. It was just planned online.

Another popular theory is that e-commerce began in late August 1994, when Pizza Hut began selling pizza online. Although this was probably the beginning of large-scale

(continued on the next page)

(continued from the previous page)

e-commerce, and it definitely had the biggest influence on the exponential growth of the e-commerce industry, it wasn't the first example of an online transaction.

It is generally agreed that the first secure online transaction was made on August 11, 1994, when Dan Kohn sold a copy of Sting's album *Ten Summoner's Tales* for $12.48 plus shipping. The sale was made through the website NetMarket, which Kohn founded and described as "the equivalent of a shopping mall in cyberspace." Now such websites are common, but back then the idea was so groundbreaking that it actually required users to download a special browser that allowed them to make these transactions.

Not only was pizza one of the first things sold online but e-commerce has now become one of the main ways pizza is sold.

WHAT DO THEY DO?

What a computer systems analyst will do for a company depends entirely on that company's needs. She may need to set up an entire IT system from scratch, she may be brought in to upgrade an existing system, or her role may simply be to troubleshoot or teach new users how to operate the system. Here are five of the main tasks involved in the job.

CONSULT

Like developers, the computer systems analyst's first step is always to consult with the management of the company to determine what it needs. Different companies require different things from their computer systems. Some e-commerce businesses operate out of a physical office where all of their employees work, while others are based online with employees scattered across the globe. These different setups have a huge effect on what kind of system will be the best fit.

Once the analyst learns what the company wants its computer system to do, she can use that information to figure out what sort of hardware it should be running and what combination of software will best suit its needs.

RESEARCH

Part of the computer systems analyst's job is to keep up to date with the latest technologies, so she will always be researching and reading up on the newest advancements, upgrades, and releases, but once she is assigned a job and she knows what sort of system she'll be working on, her research becomes a lot more specific. She searches for solutions to the company's problems, figures out how/if those solutions could fit into the company's system, and measures up the costs and benefits of the solutions to determine whether they are financially worthwhile.

IMPLEMENT

Once she has determined the ideal system for a company to run, the computer systems analyst's next step is to set up that system. This involves purchasing hardware and installing it correctly so that all the computers and accessories are properly connected. It also means acquiring software. This can be as simple as buying already-existing software out of the box, or it can include working alongside developers to create new software for the company. Some computer systems analysts are even web developers themselves and use their own programming skills to make software for their systems. Once the software is acquired, it needs to be installed and properly synced with the other programs in the system.

TEST

This is another step that computer systems analysts share with developers. Once the system has been

The computer systems analyst's job is never done. Even after a system is fully installed, it can always be upgraded as new technology is developed.

installed, it needs to be tested to ensure it works as intended. If even one cord is plugged into the wrong socket or if a program is installed on the wrong computer, it can mess up the whole system. Often it is easy to tell that something is wrong with the system. The difficult part is figuring out what is causing the problem. Sometimes these problems are easy to fix, and other times they require significant upheaval to the system.

TRAIN

Finally, once the system is in place and operating correctly, the computer systems analyst is sometimes tasked with teaching the company's staff how to use the technology. If a lot of new software has been introduced, it can take a while for employees to get the hang of using it. Because computer systems analysts have such a thorough understanding of how their systems work, they are the perfect people to educate the users on how to operate them correctly. This can take the form of dedicated training seminars with larger groups or one-on-one sessions with employees who are having specific issues with the system.

HOW TO PREPARE

The first thing to do if you want to become a computer systems analyst is to start learning about the latest technology and how systems work. Joining your school's computer or technology club can be a fun way to begin developing an understanding of these concepts. Your school may offer computer science, electronics, or other technology-based classes, which can also help to lay a foundation for further studies.

Outside of school, you can always start doing your own research, reading articles and tutorials online or in magazines. There are millions of resources out there to help you start learning. At home, you could offer to set up your mom's new computer or hook

Computer clubs are a great way to gain a better understanding of technology, with help from your friends and guidance from a teacher.

up the new internet connection. Over the summer, there are many computer and technology camps where you can be immersed in the world of computer systems.

ACCREDITATION

Most computer systems analyst jobs require at least a bachelor's degree in a computer-related field. That includes subjects such as computer science, computer information systems, management information systems, and programming.

Because computer systems analysts are required to do cost-benefit analysis and guarantee return on investment, it can also be useful to take classes in business. Some companies even prefer applicants to have a master's degree in business administration. This is particularly the case with e-commerce as the analyst needs to understand the industry for which she is building computer systems—in this case, business.

Like developers, it is important for computer systems analysts to continue their education throughout their careers, whether it be through classes or personal research. There are always new and innovative technologies being developed, and computer systems analysts need to be aware of them so that they can incorporate them into their systems and be as efficient as possible.

JOB OUTLOOK

In 2015, the Bureau of Labor Statistics projected that the number of computer systems analyst jobs in the United States would rise by 21 percent between 2014 and 2024. Though that's not quite as much of an increase as that projected for web development jobs, it is still a huge growth, far surpassing the average rate. So, if you choose to become a computer systems analyst, your skills will be in high demand.

LANDING THE PERFECT JOB

I t's one thing to have the skills and qualifications required to perform a job, but it's a whole other thing to actually secure a job in your chosen field. Finding employment can be a long and demoralizing process, but there are certain things you can do to speed up the job search and give yourself an edge when beginning your career in e-commerce.

RÉSUMÉ

Before you even begin looking for jobs, you need to get your résumé together. If you've never done this before, it can be a bit of a challenge. The first step is to write down a list of all your skills, interests, and experiences. Include everything relevant to the sort of job you're looking for: classes you've taken, specific assignments you've done, clubs you've been a part of, personal projects you've created, conventions you've attended, subjects you've done research on, and anything else you can think of.

Once you've got everything down, then it's time to structure it all into the résumé format. There are plenty of resources online, like VisualCV and

Always get someone else to look over your résumé before you send it off. There's usually at least one mistake that you don't catch on your own.

HowToWriteAResume.net, that show you what your résumé should look like. Before you send your résumé off to potential employers, make sure you show it to someone you trust. He or she might have advice for how you could better present yourself, he or she could think of an important achievement that you forgot to include, or he or she might catch a pesky typo that you missed.

In addition to a résumé, most jobs will also require a cover letter. This is where you can let your personality shine through and expand on how your skills and experience will be beneficial to the company to which you are applying. It's important to note that while you may have a generalized résumé and cover letter, you will want to look back over both of them before applying to each job and tailor them to fit the specific position for which you are applying.

NETWORKING

It's not just what you know that's going to get you a job. Who you know is just as important. Whether you like it or not, having some sort of connection to the company you're applying to will definitely give you a better chance of getting the job. That isn't just the case in e-commerce; it's the same in every industry around the world. That's why it's so important to start networking as soon as possible.

An easy way to start is by creating a LinkedIn account. Fill in your skills and interests, post about your opinions and all the new things you're learning, and start connecting with people in the industry. This is a great way to learn from people with established careers in e-commerce while also getting on their radar for job opportunities.

Other ways to connect with people include posting on forums like Stack Overflow; going to conventions, seminars, and workshops; and attending computer or technology camps. Make sure you keep in touch with the people you meet in all of these places—your peers and classmates as well as your tutors and mentors. You never know when one of them could be in the position to help you get a job.

Another thing to consider doing is contacting companies you would potentially like to work for. If you ask them about what sort of people they usually hire and what they look for in a candidate, they will usually be generous with information and advice. Not only will this help you learn what is required to get a job in the industry but it will also make the people at these companies aware of you and potentially make them more likely to offer you a job in the future.

APPLYING FOR JOBS

Once you've got your résumé ready and have talked to a few people in the industry, it's time to start applying for jobs. And where do you find jobs? On the internet. You will definitely be able to find e-commerce jobs on the generic employment sites like Monster or Indeed, but there are other more specialized sites that will make your search easier.

One of the biggest tech job websites is Dice. Like Indeed, it aggregates job listings from all over the internet and puts them all in one place for you. Other good places to look for jobs in tech are LinkedIn (because you already have an account from when you were networking) and GitHub, which, in addition to being a hosting service, also has a job listings section.

But even better than all of those options are sites like PowerToFly and Tech Ladies, which specifically aim to get women into jobs at tech companies. In addition to offering job listings, these sites offer resources to help women in all stages of their tech careers and even host events to help women network and learn from each other.

Getting to know people in your field is just as important as your computer skills, so take every opportunity to form relationships with people in the industry.

Another approach to finding an e-commerce job is to sign up with a recruitment agency. These companies will connect you directly with organizations that might be a good fit for you, meaning you don't have to spend all that time scrolling through job listings. There are even some recruitment agencies that specialize in e-commerce, like eCommerce Placement and Ecommerce Recruiter.

INTERVIEWING

If you get invited to interview for a job, you're definitely on the right track. It means the company is interested in you and wants to learn more about you. Interviews can be nerve-racking, but remember that you're there because the company thinks you would be good for the job. And remember, there are a lot of people who didn't make it as far as you.

There are a few different types of interviews—including in person, phone, online, and group interviews—but you should prepare for all of them the same way. You want to be well presented and dressed in professional clothing. When an interview is taking place over Skype or FaceTime, it can be tempting to wear a nice top and then just pajama bottoms, but it's not worth the risk. What if you have to stand up to get something during the interview? Also, if the interview is happening online or over the phone, make sure you have a good connection and you're in a quiet environment where you won't be disturbed. You don't want your little brother busting in when you're talking about how good you are at working from home.

CREATING YOUR OWN JOB

One of the great things about e-commerce is that it makes it easier to work for yourself. You don't have to worry about the application and interview process if you start your own business selling things online. There are thousands of online platforms that allow you to start making money right away.

Most people just use eBay to get rid of their old belongings that they don't want anymore, but some people make a living selling items on the site, whether it be products they are reselling for a profit or things they've made themselves. There are a lot of other sites out there through which you can sell products, like Etsy, Big Cartel, and Storenvy. There are even sites like CafePress and Zazzle that allow you to design products and then produce them on demand whenever someone purchases one.

Other platforms that allow you to become your own e-commerce vendor are websites and apps that let you sell your services, rather than physical goods. This category includes well-known platforms like Uber and Airbnb, as well as Fiverr, on which you can list any task you're willing to do for five or more dollars.

These examples are just the beginning of how you can work for yourself using e-commerce. There are new platforms popping up all the time, and if you find enough success through one of these services, you could even start your own website and do it all yourself.

No matter what type of interview it is, you should take plenty of time to prepare. Read over the original job listing, and take note of what responsibilities the job entails and what skills the company is looking for in applicants. Check any further correspondence you've had with the company so that you can be confident you're not forgetting anything important.

A smile and a confident handshake can go a long way in a face-to-face interview.

And look over your résumé and cover letter again because the interviewer may ask you about things you mentioned there.

Sometimes the company will send you the interview questions beforehand. In this case, make sure you read them carefully and practice your answers. It can be a good idea to run through your answers with someone else for practice. But whether or not you are given the questions in advance, you need to be prepared to be flexible. You never know exactly what will be asked of you during a job interview, so be ready for the unexpected.

Chapter six

YOU'VE GOT THE JOB. NOW WHAT?

Getting the job is only the first step. You still have a whole career in e-commerce ahead of you. No two careers are the same, even if they look similar to outsiders. Everyone has her own experiences, struggles, and successes in the workplace.

DIFFERENT WORK ENVIRONMENTS

Not every job in e-commerce has the same kind of work environment. Even working the same job in a different department can entail a completely different workplace. Depending on your position, you might have your own office, be in a group space, work from home, or move between different locations.

SHARED OFFICE

A shared office space is an environment like no other. While the TV show *The Office* is an exaggeration, there will still be a lot of personalities and office politics that you'll need to navigate. When you first start working in an office, it's important to get to know the other people with whom you're sharing the

Reach out to your coworkers and ask if you can join them for lunch sometime. You can learn a lot learn from someone who's been at the company longer than you.

space. Introduce yourself and be friendly. Perhaps go to lunch with them. If you can develop strong relationships with your coworkers, you'll catch on to the culture more quickly and have a much easier time in the office.

On the flip side, you need to remember that the office is not a social space. You're there to do your job. So don't let your workmates distract you from your tasks, or your boss might have something to say about it. Present yourself professionally, just like you did at your interview, and try to be a few minutes early to work each day.

WORKING FROM HOME

Though working from home has some serious advantages over going in to an office every day, it also has a few of its own challenges. Yes, it offers you more flexibility; you can wear what you want, sit on the couch or lie in bed with your laptop, and structure your work hours around other aspects of your life. But it doesn't mean complete freedom. You'll still need to be available during office hours to take phone and video calls and respond to time-sensitive emails and messages.

It can also be difficult to stay motivated when working from home. It's easy for a five-minute coffee break to turn into an hour of watching TV when there's no one around to keep you on task. And household chores can often distract you from your paid work. If you're going to be working from home regularly, it's important to establish a routine and

If you work from home, make sure you leave the house every day, even if it's just taking your laptop out into the backyard to work in the sun for a while.

a workspace somewhere in your house. This will help you focus on the task at hand. Another tip is to get dressed as if you were going in to the office. It's a lot easier to slack off when you're just wearing sweatpants and a hoodie.

CONTINUED LEARNING

E-Commerce, like all tech industries, is constantly evolving as new technologies are developed. If you don't keep up with them, you could quickly be left behind. Luckily, you will always be learning on the job. Every project and assignment is different and will bring new challenges. It's important to take these challenges in stride and learn from them so the next time you are faced with a similar situation you will know how to deal with it immediately.

Some companies offer their employees opportunities to upskill. Sometimes this takes the form of onsite seminars or workshops, or perhaps the company will pay for you to attend conferences or classes outside of work. You should make the most of these opportunities whenever they become available to you. Not only will the things you learn help you succeed in your current job, but they could also help you secure a promotion or a new job in the future.

In fact, if you want to have a long career in e-commerce, you should be making the time to continue your education, even if your company doesn't provide the opportunities for you. There is a new batch of graduates entering the workforce every

There's always more to learn when it comes to e-commerce. Many professionals find continuing education classes useful.

year, and they are trained in the newest concepts and technology. Though your experience in the workplace counts for something, you need to stay up to date on the latest industry standards so that you don't get passed over for someone with a more recent qualification.

GENDER GAPS IN THE WORKPLACE

According to the Institute for Women's Policy Research, women earned on average 20 percent less than men in 2015. This trend exists just as much in the technology industry as it does in other sectors. In a 2017 report, Hired analyzed the pay data of the tech industry and found huge discrepancies between genders. Sixty-three percent of the time, women were offered less pay than men for the same job at the same company. The average offer to women was 4 percent less than the amount offered to men in the same roles, with some companies offering up to 50 percent less. The situation is even worse for women of color and those who identify as LGBTQIA+. In fact, not only are black and LGBTQIA+ women the lowest paid of any demographic but they also have lower expectations of what salary they will be offered.

These gender gaps aren't just limited to pay. In a 2017 article for CNBC, Shawn M. Carter writes that 53 percent of the time, tech companies interviewed only male candidates for a position. So, although 74 percent of female students expressed interest in computer science, women held only 25 percent of computing jobs. The ratios get even worse in leadership positions, with only 11 percent of executive roles in Silicon Valley being held by women. This leads to websites like Zulily, which market exclusively to women and yet are run by men. It's no wonder that companies with women in leadership positions are 15 percent more profitable on average.

FEMALE ROLE MODELS

Although evidence shows that companies with diverse employees are more successful, the tech industry is still male dominated. This makes it even more important to identify female role models, leaders, and peers to provide you with inspiration and support as you navigate your way through your career. Here are a few examples of women who are leading the way and finding success in e-commerce.

KIMBERLY SMITH

Kimberly Smith is the founder and CEO of Marjani, a website dedicated to selling beauty products made for women of color. Smith was formerly an attorney but decided to start the site when she became frustrated by the lack of makeup in shades that match or complement black skin. Not only does Marjani stock makeup designed for people of color but the brands it carries are predominantly black-owned independent companies, and all the models on the site are either black, Asian, or Latina. Smith wants young women to see themselves represented when they look at Marjani, so not only is she finding success for herself but she's also supporting her community.

HOLLY TUCKER AND SOPHIE CORNISH

Holly Tucker and Sophie Cornish are responsible for the UK-based webstore Notonthehighstreet

.com, which sells original and personalized products made by more than five thousand creative small businesses. After realizing that the people who ran those small businesses needed a better platform for getting their products out into the world and that customers were always looking for unique finds, they left their careers in media and started the website with their own savings. They didn't make a profit for the first two years, but the company made £155 million in sales in 2015, and it has helped some of its small partners reach over one million pounds in sales.

KATIA BEAUCHAMP AND HAYLEY BARNA

Katia Beauchamp and Hayley Barna met at Harvard Business School and cofounded the subscription service Birchbox. For ten dollars a month, subscribers receive a personalized box of beauty and grooming product samples and the opportunity to buy full-sized versions of the products at a discount. Birchbox has been a huge success, with more than one million subscribers and more than eight hundred brand partners as of 2015, when it was valued at $485 million. The company helped start the subscription service craze, which has exploded since Birchbox's launch in 2010.

Birchbox founders Katia Beauchamp and Hayley Barna are just two examples of women thriving in e-commerce. You could be the next success story!

YOU!

Just by showing an interest in e-commerce and reading this book, you are helping to break down barriers for women to succeed in tech. Even if you don't decide to pursue a career in e-commerce, you now have a better understanding of the industry and can offer support to others who are more interested in it.

If you do decide you want to work in e-commerce, your presence will help normalize the idea that women have just as much of a place in the tech industry as men, and you will be opening up a path for other women to follow after you. There will be challenges, but by facing them you will make those same situations easier for women in the future. Your career in e-commerce will not only be rewarding on a personal level but it will also benefit other female market research analysts, web developers, and computer systems analysts. And that is certainly something to be applauded.

Glossary

CODE Instructions for computers written in programming languages.

COMPUTER SYSTEM The combination of software, hardware, and accessories that a company uses.

COMPUTER SYSTEMS ANALYST A job that involves making sure that companies are running the most efficient and profitable computer systems.

CROWDFUNDING Online platforms that allow users to invest in or donate to projects.

DATA Information, often in the form of numbers.

DEVELOPER A job that involves building and updating e-commerce platforms using code.

E-COMMERCE The sale of goods or services or any other monetary transaction that takes place online.

GENDER GAP The difference in pay and job opportunities between women and men.

GOODS Physical products.

HARDWARE The physical components of a computer.

IT Information technology or the use of computers.

MARKET RESEARCH ANALYST A job that involves analyzing data to determine how businesses can better attract customers.

PLATFORM A website or app that allows e-commerce transactions to take place

SOFTWARE Computer programs, apps, and operating systems.

TRANSACTION The process of transferring money from one person or entity to another.

TROUBLESHOOT To fix problems or errors.

VENDOR A person or company that sells a product or service.

WEBSTORE An online store.

WIREFRAMING Designing what an app or website will look like and how its pages will fit together.

For More Information

Codecademy
49 West 27th Street, 4th Floor
New York, NY 10001
http://www.codecademy.com
Facebook, Instagram, and Twitter: @codecademy
Codecademy is an online platform that offers free
   coding classes to anyone. It has over forty-five
   million users.

Girls Who Code
28 West 23rd Street
New York, NY 10010
(646) 629-9735
http://www.girlswhocode.com
Facebook, Instagram, and Twitter: @Girlswhocode
Girls Who Code is a nonprofit organization
   dedicated to teaching young women how to
   code through clubs, camps, and other programs.

National Center for Women & Information
Technology
College of Engineering & Applied Science
NCWIT
1111 Engineering Drive, ECCE 1B-36
Boulder, CO 80309
(303) 735-6671
http://www.ncwit.org
Facebook and Twitter: @ncwit
A nonprofit community that aims to increase the

participation of all women in computing fields.

PowerToFly
100 Crosby Street, Suite 308
New York, NY 10012
hi@powertofly.com
http://www.powertofly.com
Facebook, Instagram, and Twitter:
@powertofly
A recruitment agency that works to increase
    diversity and inclusion in *Fortune* 500 companies
    and startups.

Society for Canadian Women in Science and
Technology
#311—525 Seymour Street
Vancouver, BC V6B 3H7
Canada
(604) 893-8657
http://www.scwist.ca
Twitter: @scwist
A not-for-profit association that develops
    educational programs as well as networking
    and mentorship opportunities to encourage
    women to begin and continue careers in science,
    engineering, and technology.

TechGirls Canada
hello@techgirls.ca
http://www.techgirls.ca
Twitter: @techgirlscan
Facebook: @techgirlscanada
TechGirls Canada is a national organization that
connects hundreds of nonprofit and industry
groups with the goal of encouraging more young
women to pursue careers in technology.

Tech Ladies
help@hiretechladies.com
http://www.hiretechladies.com
Facebook: @therealTechLadies
Instagram: @tech.ladies
Twitter: @HireTechLadies
A worldwide organization that helps women find
jobs in the technology industry. It has more than
twenty thousand members.

For Further Reading

Deutsch, Stacia. *The Friendship Code #1*. New York, NY: Penguin Workshop, 2017.

Hand, Carol. *Careers for Tech Girls in Technology*. New York, NY: Rosen Publishing, 2016.

Harmon, Daniel. *Powering Up a Career in Software Development and Programming*. New York, NY: Rosen Publishing, 2016.

Harris, Patricia. *Why Are There So Many Programming Languages*? New York, NY: Rosen Publishing, 2018.

La Bella, Laura. *Becoming a Systems Analyst*. New York, NY: Rosen Publishing, 2018.

Mooney, Carla. *Using Computer Science in Online Retail Careers*. New York, NY: Rosen Publishing, 2018.

Nagle, Jeanne. *Careers in Internet Advertising and Marketing*. New York, NY: Rosen Publishing, 2014.

Niver, Heather Moore. *Careers for Tech Girls in Computer Science*. New York, NY: Rosen Publishing, 2016.

Niver, Heather Moore. *Getting to Know Ruby*. New York, NY: Rosen Publishing, 2015.

Scally, Robert. *Jeff Bezos: Founder of Amazon and the Kindle*. Greensboro, NC: Morgan Reynolds, 2012.

Archer, Seth. "Companies with Women in Leadership Roles Crush the Competition." Business Insider, June 17, 2016. https://www.businessinsider.com.au/companies-with-women-in-leadership-roles-perform-better-2016-6?r=US&IR=T.

Bureau of Labor Statistics. *Occupational Outlook Handbook*. Retrieved October 3, 2017. https://www.bls.gov.

Fortini, Amanda. "How Sassy Is Tavi Gevinson?" *New York Times*, August 31, 2011. http://www.nytimes.com/2011/09/04/magazine/how-sassy-is-tavi-gevinson.html.

Fundable. "The History of Crowdfunding." Retrieved October 5, 2017. https://www.fundable.com/crowdfunding101/history-of-crowdfunding.

Grothaus, Michael. "You'll Never Guess What the First Thing Ever Sold on the Internet Was." *Fast Company*, November 26, 2015. https://www.fastcompany.com/3054025/youll-never-guess-what-the-first-thing-ever-sold-on-the-internet-was.

Guru99. "Alpha Testing Vs Beta Testing." Retrieved October 7, 2017. https://www.guru99.com/alpha-beta-testing-demystified.html.

Insights Association. "Professional Researcher Certification." Retrieved October 1, 2017. http://www.insightsassociation.org/advance-career/prc.

Institute for Women's Policy Research. "Pay Equity & Discrimination." Retrieved October 8, 2017.

https://iwpr.org/issue/employment-education
-economic-change/pay-equity-discrimination.

Interview with Rose Lu, Storypark. Wellington, New Zealand. October 7, 2017.

Kirkpatrick, Jessica. "Women, Work, and the State of Wage Inequality." Hired. Retrieved October 8, 2017. https://hired.com/gender-wage-gap-2017.

Learn.org. "What Are My Career Options in E-Commerce?" Retrieved August 25, 2017. http://learn.org/articles/E-Commerce_Careers _What_Are_My_Job_Options.html.

Liquid State. "How to Build an App: The Process Behind App Development." Best Practices, March 10, 2017. https://liquid-state.com/the -process-behind-app-development.

Luckhurst, Pheobe. "'I'm Not Good at Doing What I'm Told': Meet Real-Life Girlboss Sophia Amoruso." The Guardian, May 11, 2017. https:// www.theguardian.com/lifeandstyle/2017/may/11 /girlboss-feminism-sophia-amoruso-nasty-gal -netflix-cinderella-tech-tv-series.

Mandel, Michael. "How E-Commerce Is Raising Pay and Creating Jobs around the Country." Forbes, April 3, 2017. https://www.forbes.com /sites/realspin/2017/04/03/how-e-commerce -is-raising-pay-and-creating-jobs-around-the -country/#68e7050a6dff.

Meazy, Matt. "The Web Design Process in 7 Simple Steps." Webflow, March 13, 2017. https:// webflow.com/blog/the-web-design-process-in -7-simple-steps.

Noland, Marcus, Tyler Moran, and Barbara
    Kotschwar. "Is Gender Diversity Profitable?
    Evidence from a Global Survey." Peterson
    Institute for International Economics, February
    2016. https://piie.com/publications/wp/wp16-3
    .pdf.
Paul, Binu. "FabAlley.com Raises $2 mn Series A
    Funding." TechCircle, October 13, 2016. http://
    techcircle.vccircle.com/2016/10/13/faballey
    -com-raises-2-mn-series-a-funding.
Rodulfo, Kristina. "There's Now a Beauty
    E-Commerce Site Dedicated to Women of
    Color." *Elle*, April 13, 2017. http://www.elle.com
    /beauty/news/a44534/marjani-beauty-site
    -women-of-color.
Smith, Cooper. "The E-Commerce Demographics
    Report: In a Reversal, Women Are Now
    Dominating Mobile Shopping." Business Insider,
    September 15, 2015. http://www.businessinsider
    .com/women-are-driving-growth-in-mobile
    -commerce-heres-how-2015-090/?r=AU&IR=T.
Statista. "E-Commerce Share of Total Global
    Retail Sales from 2015 to 2021." Key Figures of
    E-Commerce. Retrieved October 1, 2017. https://
    www.statista.com/statistics/534123/e
    -commerce-share-of-retail-sales-worldwide.

Index

ABOUT THE AUTHOR

Jackson Nieuwland is a writer and editor from New Zealand. They have an MA in creative writing from the International Institute of Modern Letters. They have always been interested in technology, particularly coding and programming, but have never been confident enough to commit to learning more about it. The process of writing and researching this book has made the subject seem more accessible, and they are planning to spend more time learning to build websites.

PHOTO CREDITS

Cover Nikodash/Shutterstock.com; cover, interior pages (circuit board illustration) © iStockphoto.com/Vladgrin; p. 5 Bloomberg/Getty Images; p. 8 Casimiro PT/ Shutterstock.com; p. 10 Africa Studio/Shutterstock.com; p. 13 © iStockphoto.com/Zyabich; p. 15 dotshock /Shutterstock.com; p. 18 Maddie Meyer/Getty Images; p. 20 Foxy burrow/Shutterstock.com; pp. 22, 64–65 Cindy Ord/Getty Images; pp. 24, 45 Hero Images/Getty Images; p. 27 Georgejmclittle/Shutterstock.com; p. 29 Jacob Lund/Shutterstock.com; p. 33 Mikhail Rusanov/ Shutterstock.com; p. 25 © AP Images; p. 38 Hinterhaus Productions/Taxi/Getty Images; p. 40 YinYang/E+ /Getty Images; p. 43 Alpa Prod/Shutterstock.com; p. 48 Hill Street Studios/Blend Images/Getty Images; p. 51 Caiaimage/Sam Edwards/OJO+/Getty Images; p. 54 sturti /E+/Getty Images; p. 57 Paul Bradbury/OJO Images /Getty Images; p. 59 Paul Bradbury/Caiaimage /Getty Images; p. 61 Tom Merton/Caiaimage/Getty Images.

Design and Layout: Nicole Russo-Duca; Editor: Rachel Aimee; Photo Researcher: Karen Huang